DINOSAURS

CARNIVORES

Have an adult help you remove the stickers.

Phidal

Did You Know That?

Carnivorous dinosaurs were meat-eaters that hunted or scavenged for their food. Use your stickers to find out more about these titans of the past.

The name "dinosaur" is made of two Greek words: *deinos* (fearfully great) and *sauros* (lizard).

The jaws of the Tyrannosaurus were big enough to swallow a human whole!

Velociraptors had a sickle-shaped claw on each foot.

The Spinosaurus may have used the big sail on its back to scare off other dinosaurs.

Fossils show that the Nqwebasaurus swallowed rocks to help it digest food.

The Baryonyx is the only dinosaur known to have an appetite for fish.

The tiny Compsognathus
ate insects, small lizards,
and primitive mammals.

The Cryolophosaurus, which means
"cold crested lizard," was
found in Antarctica.

Velociraptors were fast-running
predators with hollow bones
and big brains.

The hollow bones and long legs
of a Gallimimus allowed it to
run as fast as an ostrich.

Troodons, who are thought to be the
smartest of all dinosaurs, were probably
as bright as today's birds.

The large eyes of the Leaellynasaura
helped it see better when it
hunted for food at night.

Carnivore Facts

Carnivorous dinosaurs didn't get along very well. Many of their bones have been found with bite marks made by other carnivores!

The arms of a Tyrannosaurus were so small that they couldn't even bring food to its mouth!

Scientists calculated how fast dinosaurs ran by measuring their bone lengths and fossilized footprints.

Oviraptor fossils have been found next to their nests, which could mean they guarded their babies and eggs at any cost.

The Giganotosaurus was the biggest known land carnivore.

Unlike most dinosaurs, the Sinornithosaurus had feathers instead of leathery skin.

Paleontologists dig up Allosaurus bones more often than any other carnivorous dinosaur.

Velociraptors hunted in packs because most of their prey was much larger than they were.

The Carnotaurus had knobby eyebrow horns and arms even tinier than those of the Tyrannosaurus!

The Carcharodontosaurus was a large, fierce predator that could even hunt giant herbivores.

The Bambiraptor had many bird-like features, like feathers, wing-shaped arms, and even a wishbone!

The Eoraptor was one of the oldest-known dinosaurs. It lived 228 million years ago!

The thin crest on the head of the Dilophosaurus was probably only for display, and not a weapon.

Prehistoric Predators

Carnivores relied on their strength and hunting skills for survival. Bring this scene to life with your stickers.

2-3

4-5

12

6-11

13

16

14-15

Close-Up: The T. Rex

The Tyrannosaurus rex was the most powerful carnivore to ever walk the Earth. Discover what made the T. rex the perfect predator.

Its sharp teeth were the length of bananas!

The T. rex's eyes were close together, which helped it spot its prey more easily.

It used its tail to balance the weight of its enormous head.

The small arms of a T. rex were actually three times stronger than ours!

The T. rex ran up to 25 miles per hour.

The Life Cycle of the Tyrannosaurus

Follow the life of the Tyrannosaurus to see how a young carnivore grew up to be a top predator.

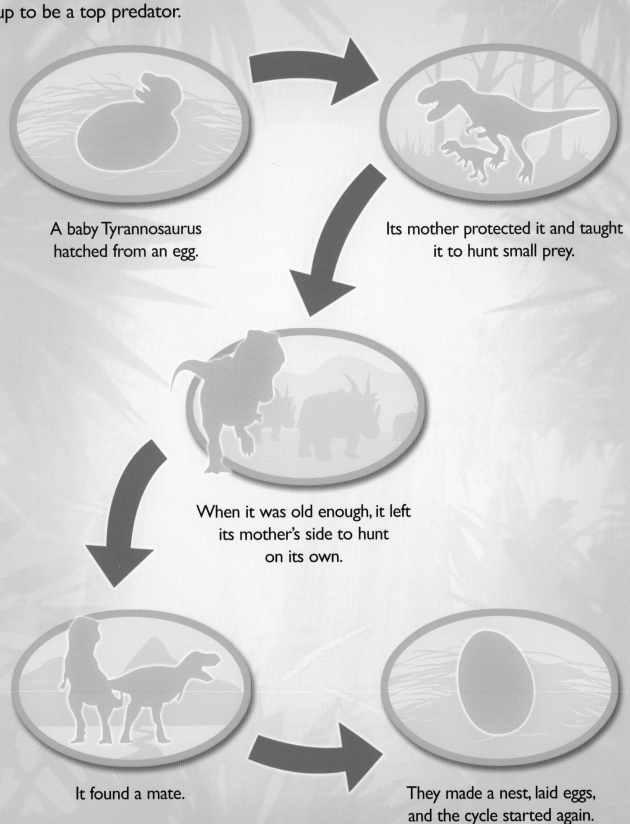

A baby Tyrannosaurus hatched from an egg.

Its mother protected it and taught it to hunt small prey.

When it was old enough, it left its mother's side to hunt on its own.

It found a mate.

They made a nest, laid eggs, and the cycle started again.

Where Were They Found?

Carnivores have been found on every continent in the world, even Antarctica!
Match your stickers with their appropriate country.

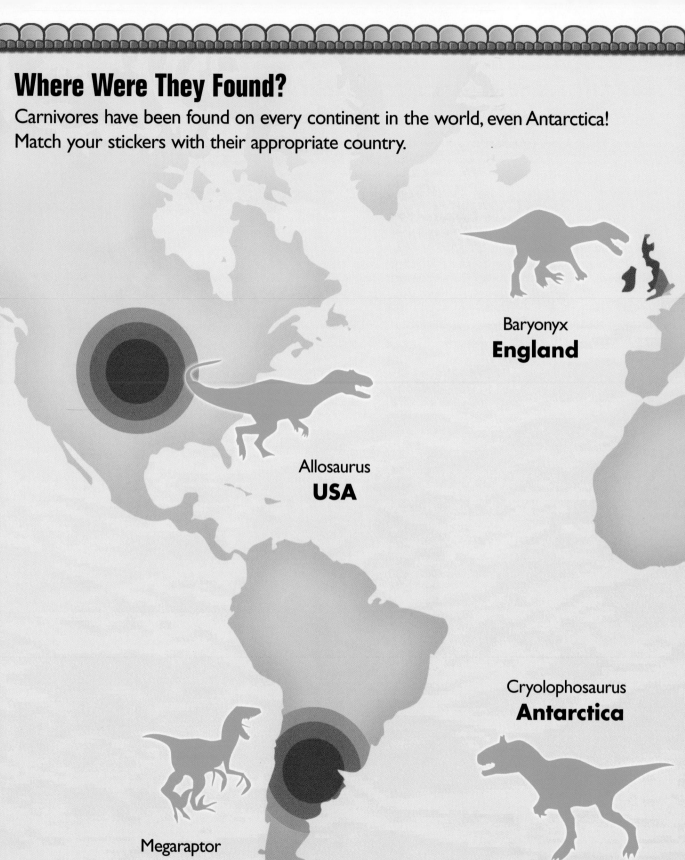

Baryonyx
England

Allosaurus
USA

Cryolophosaurus
Antarctica

Megaraptor
Argentina

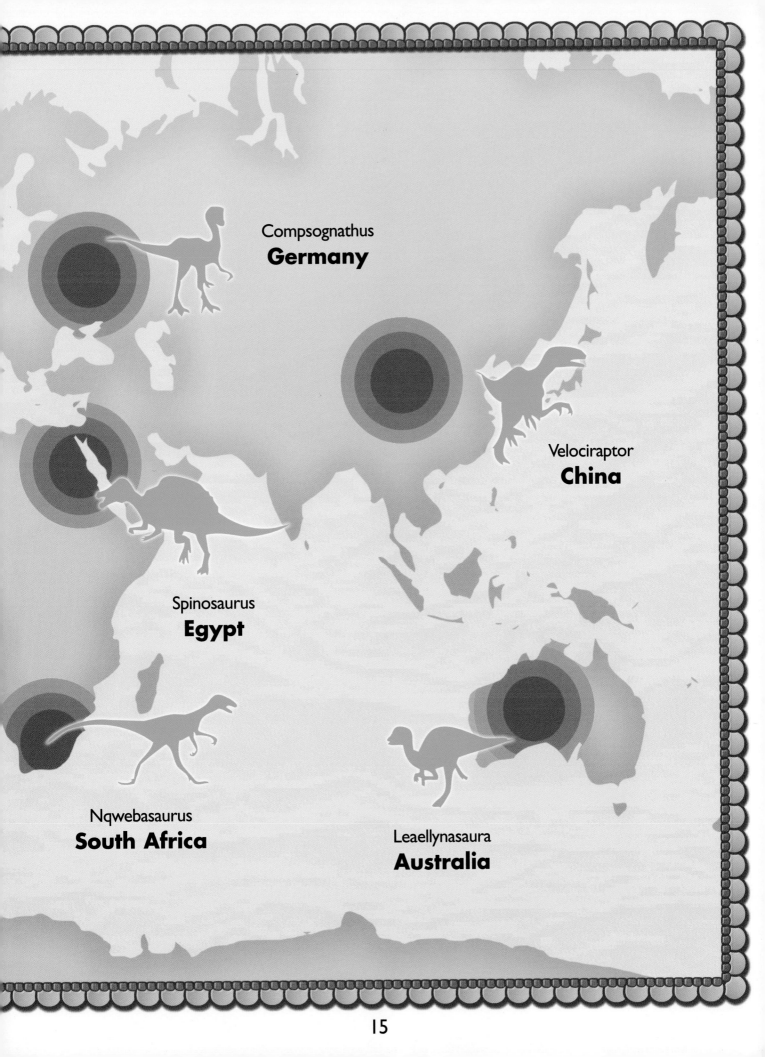

Compsognathus
Germany

Velociraptor
China

Spinosaurus
Egypt

Nqwebasaurus
South Africa

Leaellynasaura
Australia

Can You Spot...

Guess which sticker matches each of these shadows.

Carcharodontosaurus

Gallimimus

Allosaurus

Compsognathus

Bambiraptor

DINOSAURS

FLYING CREATURES

Have an adult help you remove the stickers.

Phidal

Did You Know That?

Pterosaurs shared the skies with prehistoric birds and insects during the age of the dinosaurs. Use your stickers to find out more.

Before dinosaurs ruled the Earth, insects did.

Pterosaurs were not dinosaurs or early birds. They were flying reptiles.

Many insect fossils come from pieces of fossilized tree sap called amber.

Pterosaurs had to watch out for hungry Spinosaurs.

Some pterosaurs, like the Dimorphodon, had many sharp teeth.

Other pterosaurs, like the Sordes Pilosus, were covered in fur.

Like modern pelicans, the Rhamphorhynchus would carry fish in its throat pouch to feed to its young.

Meganeura were prehistoric dragonflies that measured one foot long!

The Pterodaustro had thin, comb-like teeth similar to the modern flamingo. It was thought to be pink, too!

The Archaeopteryx, whose name means "ancient wing," is the oldest bird known to exist.

The Anurognathus, a short-tailed pterosaur, was as small as a sparrow.

The Quetzalcoatlus was the largest known pterosaur with a wingspan of up to 60 feet.

Flying Facts

Pterosaurs are the most famous of all flying creatures from prehistoric times. Get to know these ancient animals with your stickers.

The word pterosaur comes from two Greek words that mean "winged lizard."

Many pterosaurs had brightly colored crests, which were probably used to attract a mate.

Nearly all pterosaur fossils have been found near ancient seas because they used to live by the shore.

Pterosaurs had light, hollow bones.

There are two groups of pterosaurs, the long-tails and the short-tails.

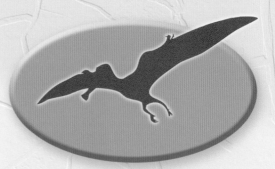

Pterosaurs did not have feathers.

Pterosaur bones are hard to find
in one piece because they often
got damaged over time.

The large wings of a pterosaur made
it awkward for it to travel
along the ground.

Pterosaurs probably flew
as fast as birds, up to
30 miles per hour.

Pterosaur remains have been
found on all the continents,
even Antarctica!

The wings of a pterosaur were made
of thin membranes attached to
two long fingers.

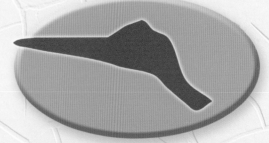

Pterosaur brains were larger
than those of any dinosaur
alive at that time.

Gone Fishing

Fish was an important food source for many pterosaurs. Bring this seaside scene to life with your stickers.

2-3

4-5

6-11

14-15

13

12

16

Bizarre Beaks!

Pterosaur heads and beaks came in a variety of peculiar shapes. Can you match your pterosaur stickers to their beaks below?

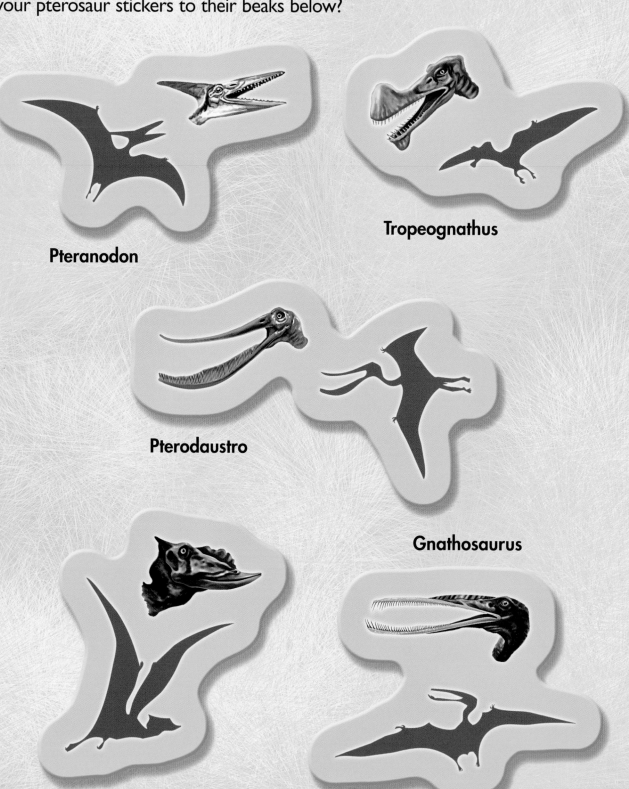

Pteranodon

Tropeognathus

Pterodaustro

Gnathosaurus

Dsungaripterus

Wingspan Match-Up

The size of a pterosaur is measured by its wingspan, or the length of its wings. Use your stickers to uncover the biggest of them all!

Anurognathus
1 foot

Pterodactylus
2 feet

Dimorphodon
6 feet

Dsungaripterus
10 feet

Pteranodon
30 feet

Quetzalcoatlus
40 to 60 feet

On the Hunt

A hungry Pteranodon is searching for food. Fly through this dinosaur land with your stickers to help her catch her dinner.

A female Pteranodon scouts
the coast for a meal.

From high up, she spots a fish
near the water's surface.

She dives into the water at high
speed and scoops up the fish
in her large beak.

Using her wings, she propels
herself to the surface . . .

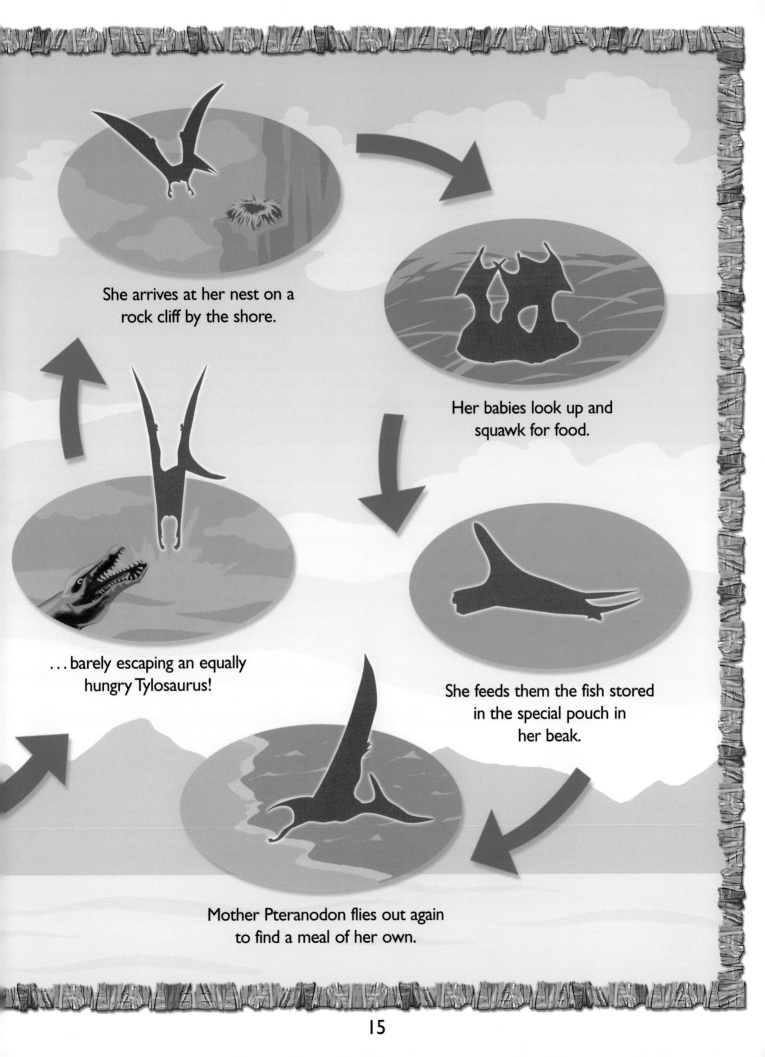

She arrives at her nest on a
rock cliff by the shore.

Her babies look up and
squawk for food.

... barely escaping an equally
hungry Tylosaurus!

She feeds them the fish stored
in the special pouch in
her beak.

Mother Pteranodon flies out again
to find a meal of her own.

Can You Spot...
Guess which sticker matches each of these shadows.

Meganeura

Archaeopteryx

Sordes Pilosus

Gnathosaurus

Quetzalcoatlus

DINOSAURS

HERBIVORES

Have an adult help you remove the stickers.

Phidal

Did You Know That?

Dinosaurs that ate only plants are called herbivores. Use your stickers to find out more about these prehistoric giants.

The largest dinosaur bones ever found belong to gigantic Sauropods.

The first dinosaur bones found back in the early 1800s came from an Iguanodon.

Despite its enormous size, the Stegosaurus had a brain the size of a walnut.

Triceratops, whose name means "three-horned face," had the largest horns of any dinosaur.

The Ankylosaur holds the record as the widest dinosaur.

The dome-headed Pachycephalosaurus may have used its thick skull for head-butting.

The Einiosaurus was a herd animal that traveled in a large group.

The Diplodocus grew longer than a tennis court, but its head was smaller than a tennis racket.

While the Brachiosaurus stood 50 feet tall, it hatched from an egg the size of a football.

The Euoplocephalus had a large, club-like tail that it used against its enemies.

The Scutellosaurus walked on two and four legs.

The Micropachycephalosaurus is the dinosaur with the longest name.

Herbivore Facts

Herbivores always had to be on the lookout for predators. Learn about their defense mechanisms and other facts with the help of your stickers.

The Diplodocus had blunt teeth made for stripping leaves off of treetops.

The Ankylosaur had heavy armor plates and spikes all over its body, even its eyelids!

A Stegosaurus defended itself by whipping its spiked tail at attacking predators.

The Massospondylus may have used its hands for grasping, as well as walking.

Some duck-billed Hadrosaurs had 960 teeth. That's more than any other dinosaur!

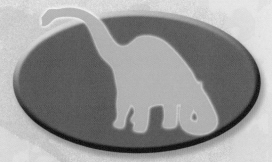

The heaviest dinosaur of all was the Argentinosaurus, who weighed over 100 tons.

The hollow crest of a Lambeosaurus was often bigger than the rest of its skull.

The Sauroposeidon is the tallest dinosaur yet discovered. It was as tall as a six-storey building.

While the Apatosaurus and the Brontosaurus were thought to be different species, they are in fact the same dinosaur.

The Parasaurolophus may have made sounds with the crest on its head to warn the herd of danger.

Although it looked like a carnivore, the Nothronychus was actually a plant-eater.

Some herbivores like the Diplodocus swallowed large stones to help grind up the food in their stomachs.

The Plains

Many herbivores roamed the plains to find food high and low. Bring this scene to life with your stickers.

13

12

16

6-11

2-3

4-5

14-15

Match the Teeth

The shape of an herbivore's teeth determined what it ate, from tough bark to soft fruit. Use your stickers to match these dinosaurs with their teeth.

The Diplodocus had peg-like teeth.

The Stegosaurus had leaf-shaped teeth.

The Triceratops had many flat cheek teeth.

The Iguanodon had curved and notched teeth.

The Ankylosaur had hand-shaped teeth.

What Did They Eat?

Herbivores ate a wide variety of plants, depending on their body type. Find out what each of these dinosaurs ate with your stickers.

The Iguanodon
ate leaves.

The Brachiosaurus
ate treetops.

The Torosaurus ate
flowering plants.

The Pachycephalosaurus
ate fruit.

The Corythosaurus
ate pine needles.

Defense Mechanisms

A Tyrannosaurus is on the prowl for a tasty herbivore. Help these dinosaurs protect themselves by matching the stickers with their defenses.

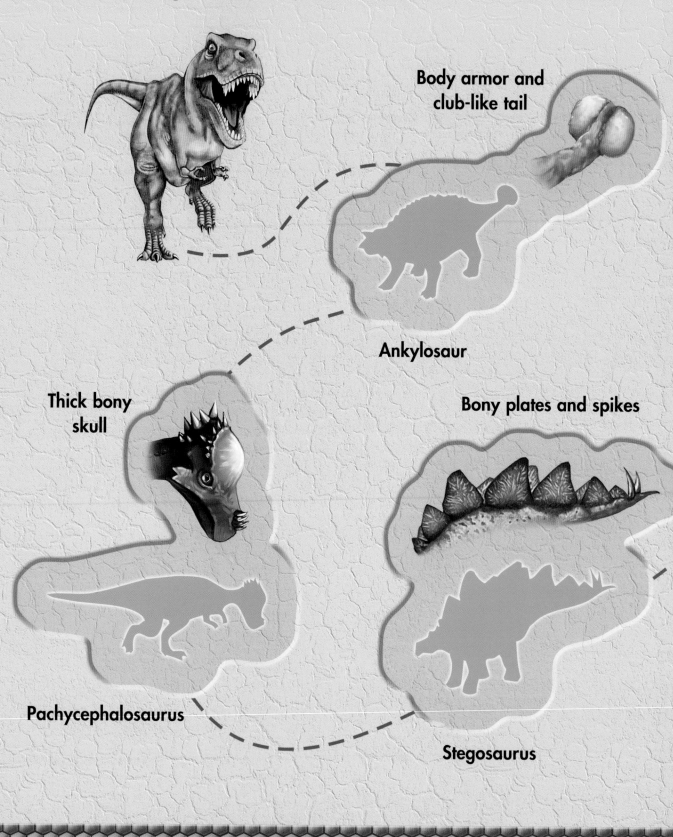

Body armor and club-like tail

Ankylosaur

Thick bony skull

Bony plates and spikes

Pachycephalosaurus

Stegosaurus

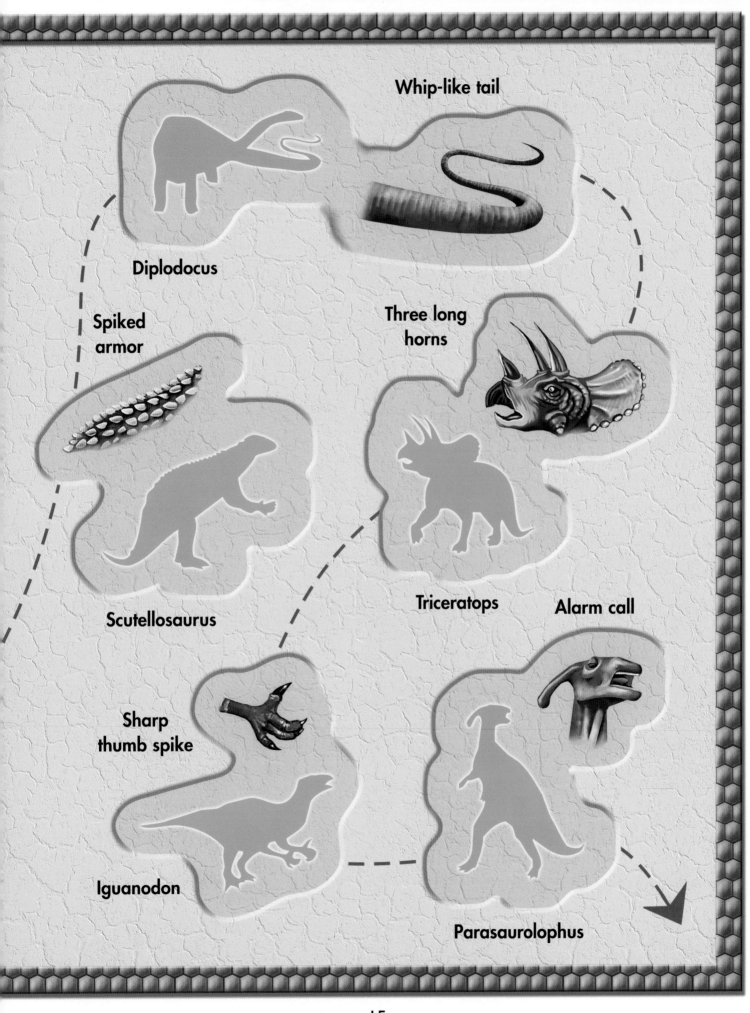

Whip-like tail

Diplodocus

Spiked armor

Three long horns

Scutellosaurus

Triceratops

Alarm call

Sharp thumb spike

Iguanodon

Parasaurolophus

Can You Spot...

Guess which sticker matches each of these shadows.

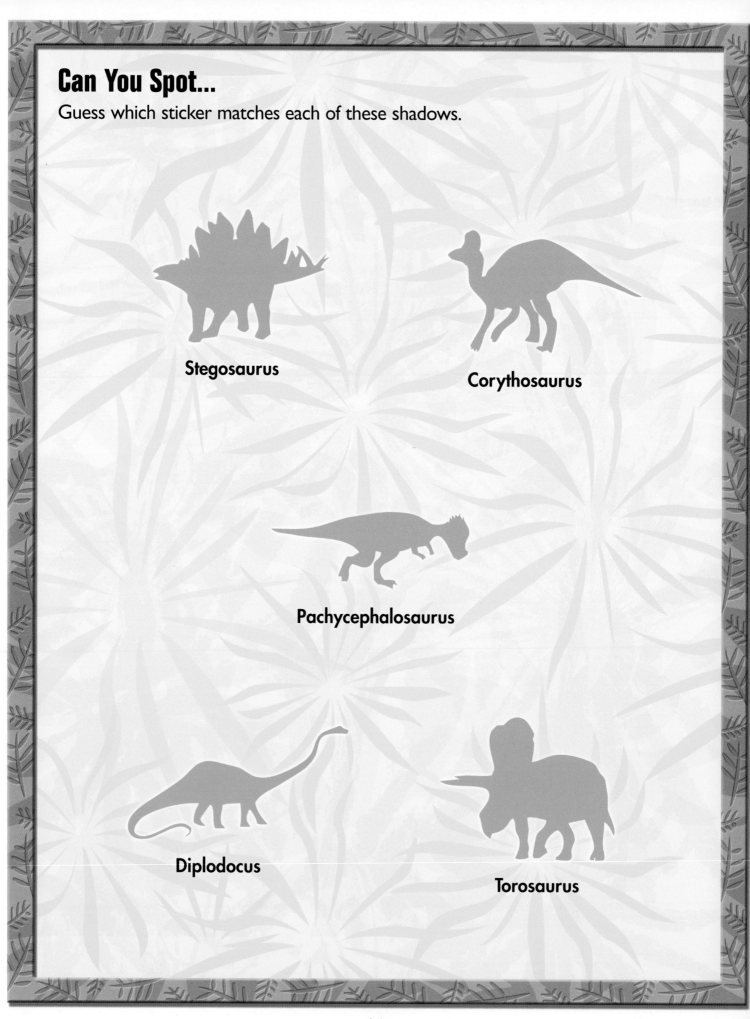

Stegosaurus

Corythosaurus

Pachycephalosaurus

Diplodocus

Torosaurus

SEA CREATURES

Have an adult help you remove the stickers.

Did You Know That?

An amazing variety of underwater reptiles, fish, and amphibians lived during prehistoric times. Get to know these creatures of the deep with your stickers.

Before the time of the dinosaurs, the sea was filled with primitive creatures called Carpoids.

Agnathans were the earliest fish species. Their mouths never closed because they had no jaws.

The Hybodus was an ancestor of the shark. The males had barbed horns on their heads.

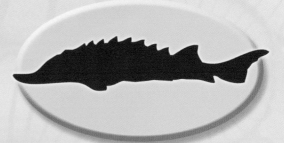

Sturgeons first appeared 250 million years ago and are still around today.

Archelons were giant turtles that grew to be as big as cars.

The Woolungasaurus used its fins to propel through the water the way penguins do today.

The head of the Kronosaurus was 10 feet long!

The Elasmosaurus had 72 vertebrae in its long neck, more than any other marine reptile.

The Liopleurodon's teeth were twice as long as the T. rex's, making it the king of the underwater food chain.

Mosasaurs had snake-like tongues which they used to detect an animal's scent in water.

The Ichthyosaur was an ancient reptile that looked a lot like the modern dolphin.

The Stethacanthus had an unusual anvil-shaped dorsal fin.

Underwater Facts

While dinosaurs ruled the land, gigantic and dangerous marine animals called the seas their home. Use your stickers to find out more.

All sea reptiles had lungs, not gills. They had to come up to the surface for air.

The Tylosaurus used its flippers to chase its prey with speed.

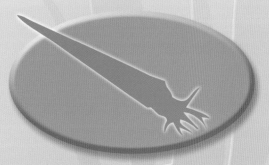

The Orthocone swam by pushing a jet of water out of its body.

At 65 feet long, the Giant Ichthyosaur was the largest marine reptile.

Crocodiles actually lived in prehistoric times.

The Diplocaulus was an amphibian that hunted on the land and in the water.

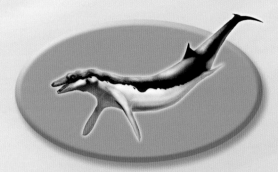

The Basilosaurus was an air-breathing
mammal, much like the
whales of today.

At 50 feet, the Megalodon was
more than twice the size of
a Great White shark.

Long before sea reptiles, the six-foot
long Pterygotus was the
king of the sea.

The heavy armor plating that covered
the Dunkleosteus made it look like
it was wearing a helmet.

The Leedsichthys was a gentle giant
that lived on tiny shrimps,
jellyfish, and plankton.

Trilobites were simple marine
animals that filtered mud
to find food.

Sea Life

While dinosaurs roamed the Earth, sea reptiles were kings of the deep. Bring this scene to life with your stickers.

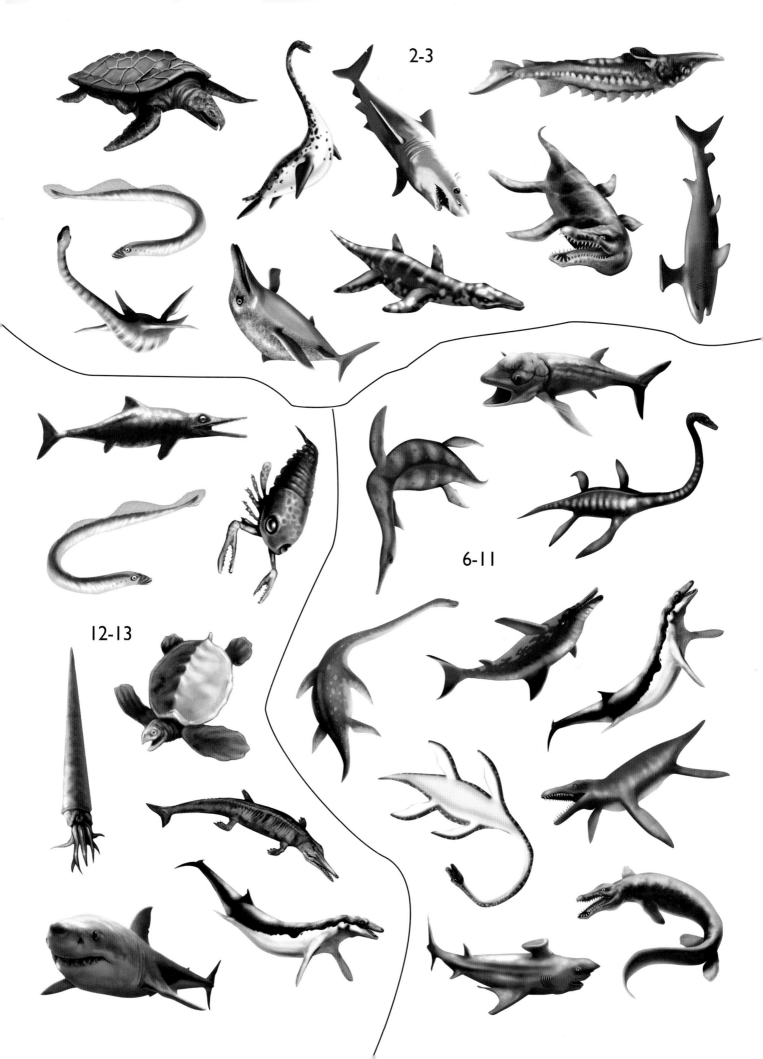

2-3

6-11

12-13

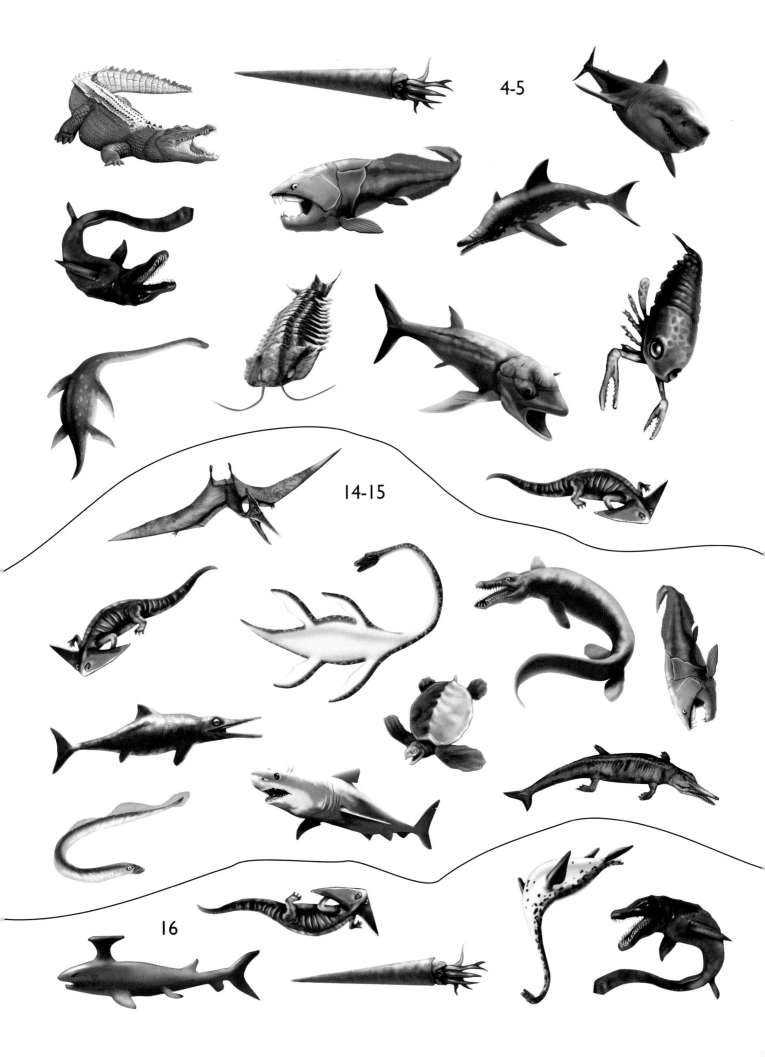

What Did They Look Like?

Many modern-day sea creatures had giant distant relatives in prehistoric times.
Can you match up these similar animals?

Eel

Agnathan

Shark

Megalodon

Dolphin

Ichthyosaur

Turtle

Archelon

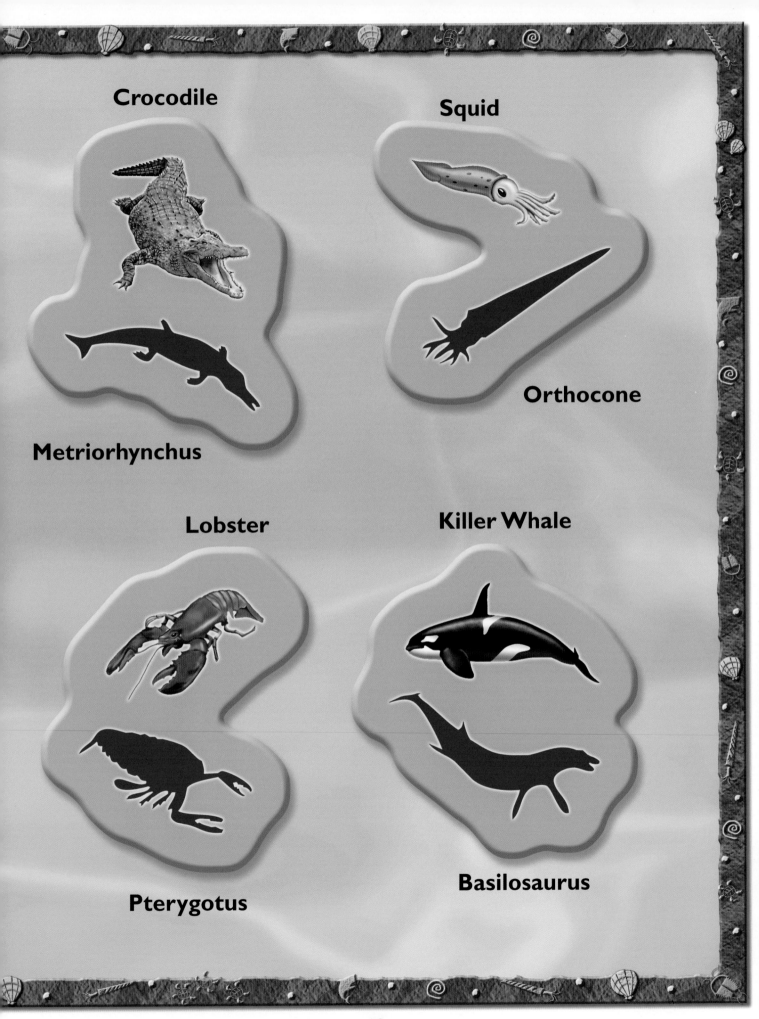

Crocodile

Squid

Metriorhynchus

Orthocone

Lobster

Killer Whale

Pterygotus

Basilosaurus

Dangerous Waters

The prehistoric sea was a scary place for small creatures. Help this little fish find a safe way home by avoiding the hungry predators.

Start

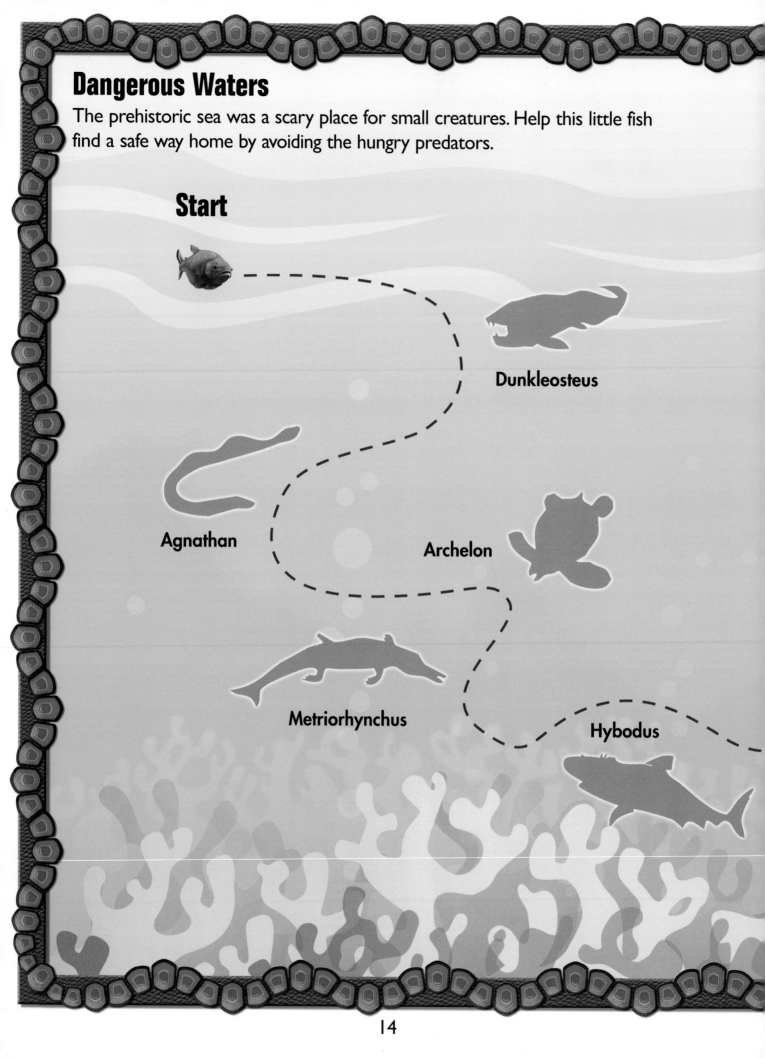

Dunkleosteus

Agnathan

Archelon

Metriorhynchus

Hybodus

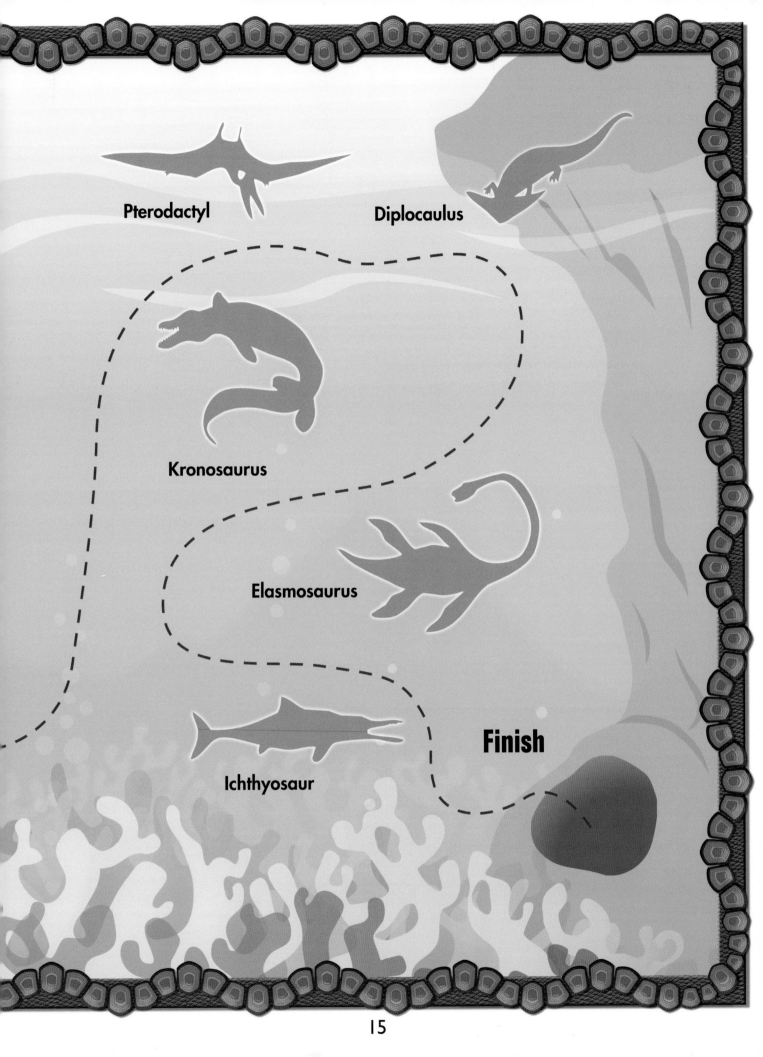

Pterodactyl

Diplocaulus

Kronosaurus

Elasmosaurus

Ichthyosaur

Finish

Can You Spot...

Guess which sticker matches each of these shadows.

Orthocone

Diplocaulus

Woolungasaurus

Stethacanthus

Kronosaurus